ABCs

FOR REDISCOVERING FAMILY CONNECTIONS

ABCs

FOR REDISCOVERING FAMILY CONNECTIONS

An Interactive Workbook for Caregivers

BETSY L. STONE, LPC, ATR

Langdon Street Press
322 First Avenue N, 5th floor
Minneapolis, MN 55401
612.455.2293
www.langdonstreetpress.com

ISBN-13: 978-1-63505-143-8
LCCN: 2016905201

Distributed by Itasca Books

Cover Design by Betsy Stone
Typeset by T. Schaeppi

Printed in the United States of America

In loving memory of my grandparents,

Lisle and Evalyn Smith,

who taught me the value of family fun and never giving up!

Contents

The ABCs

INTRODUCTION

As a therapist working with children and families for the past twenty-five-plus years, I have witnessed the magic of positive experiences changing children's and families' lives for the better. I created this book as an opportunity for caregivers to tap into that positivity, and to discover new ways of seeing and relating to their children. This book is structured in an A to Z format, with a "concept word" for each letter as well as corresponding activities. These activities will help you, the caregiver, improve the quality of family connectedness. By doing these activities, you'll find yourself interacting with your children in a more conscious and deliberate manner. As a result, your home will become happier, healthier, and more stable.

Most caregivers have moments in their lives when they are unsure how to respond to their children; for example, when the children are crying, having a temper tantrum, or are refusing to do what is being asked of them. Caregivers often feel frustrated and/or discouraged because their children are pushing their emotional buttons or stretching them beyond their comfort zones in knowing how to respond.

At different points in time, all caregivers feel overwhelmed, confused, ill equipped, and sometimes even helpless and hopeless in response to their child's actions or the life situations in which their child is exposed. Whether at home, at school, or in the community, as your child matures through the stages of development, he may be: struggling to fit in, feeling like what he says doesn't matter, questioning right from wrong, doubting what he is capable of doing, or isolating himself due to feeling upset or insecure. As a caregiver, it is only human to say, "I can't take this anymore" or "I don't know what to do." Perhaps you may feel like you have "lost your way" as a caregiver and need a helpful jump start. This book is intended to help you learn from your experiences in order to live in the present and create a healthier future.

The *ABCs* is different from other parenting books, as it's more down-to-earth and to the point. It shows you exactly how you can make a lasting difference in the lives of your children, which in turn will bless your life. It is intended as a gift to families to motivate caregivers to rediscover who your children are inside and out. I firmly believe in the value of focusing on the positives of how we can help ourselves, and how we can learn from the past. Certainly, we're not defined by how we were raised, by what may have been done to us, or by the choices we have made. Yes, we have been influenced and shaped by our past; however, as adults and as caregivers, we have the power to create our lives—and our children's lives—in a manner that feels right to us as individuals.

Day by day, you as the caregiver are intentionally or unintentionally creating your family legacy. Every moment is an opportunity to be different or better than you are today. I continue to be inspired by Gandhi, who stated, "Be the change you want to see in the world." It is up to you to decide how active you want to be in making a positive impression on your children's lives.

Caregivers with children of all ages will benefit from this book. If you are a new parent, you may be introduced to different ways of seeing how your words, actions, and the environment impact the well-being and development of your child. If you're a more experienced parent, you may be exposed to alternative ways of viewing your role as a caregiver. This book may in fact be a catalyst for reinventing who you want to be as a family.

Therapists, child development staff, educators, and mental health (MH) workers will also benefit from using this book. For persons who work directly with children or families, or both, the book can function as an educational tool and a hands-on activity resource that will engage caregivers during a session or as homework assignments. To note, having a MH professional join the process of going through this book will enrich the overall interactional experience for families.

Since we are not given an instruction manual as caregivers, it is up to each one of us as adults to craft the future; to decide if we want to live more knowledgably and deliberately than before. This book will assist that process of normalizing life's challenges and gifts as part of raising yourself and your children. We, the caregivers, have the power to do things proactively to benefit our present and future generations.

TIPS FOR USING THIS BOOK

- **A TO Z:**
  The book is constructed in an A to Z format, with each letter containing a concept word that elaborates on a specific aspect of caregiving. I invite you to identify the parenting strategies that you are already doing well; I'd also encourage you to try some of the recommended prescriptive strategies with your children. There is a brief description of each parenting concept in the "Overview of the A to Z Concepts."

- **Approach to Prescriptive Strategies:**
  I recommend that you use active listening in response to your child's input. Active listening entails listening without distractions, interruptions or judgments and then repeating back and/or clarifying what you heard your child say. This is essential to promote the transformational process to show your child that you are being more intentional and child-centered. It is also beneficial to get on your child's eye level when interacting with her. This helps your child experience your full presence when engaging with her.

- **Book Order:**
  You may choose to read this book from cover to cover, with one letter after the other **OR** jump around to concepts that speak to you **OR** pick a word at random. Any of these ways is fine.

- **"Ponder and Personalize" Words:**
  In addition to the specific assigned word, each alphabet letter has other words or phrases to ponder and personalize as part of the interactional experience, with space to journal your thoughts, feelings, and experiences. You may involve your children as much as you feel comfortable in this exploratory process.

- **A to Z Coloring Pages:**
  Each letter has its own coloring page for you, the caregiver, and/or family members

to use. These pages are located in the second half of the book, in alphabetical order. I encourage you to use a variety of art mediums to individualize these ABC pages, such as markers, crayons, collage (e.g., photos, magazine pictures, words, textured papers), watercolor (e.g., pencils, payons, or brush form), or colored pencils. Feel free to rip the coloring pages out or make copies so each family member can be a part of the process.

- **Background on the Book's Creation:**
  This section is the most technical portion of the book, so take your time if you choose to read it. It provides more food for thought on child development and the role of parental influence on children's lives, as well as my creative process as the author and illustrator.

- **Personalize:**
  You may try any or all of the prescriptive suggestions to personalize the book for your family. The recommended suggestions may be direct or indirect tasks for you, the caregiver, to do in the moment or in your home environment. Remember: this book is for your personal use, so feel free to color and write your reflections throughout the book.

- **Savor This Special Time:**
  As you explore new ways to see and be with one another, savor this time to just be with yourself or with your family. Give yourself credit for what you have done and are doing well as a parent. Be gracious and loving toward yourself as you read this book and put it into practice.

BACKGROUND ON THE BOOK'S CREATION

Our words and actions as adult caregivers have a powerful impact on the development and well-being of the children in our lives. These children may be born to you, adopted by you, or befriended by you, perhaps via someone you met at the local store, school, or playground. Your influence on these children may be greater than you're aware of—how they feel about themselves, how they get along with others, what they do with their abilities in the present and the future.

We are created as social beings who need other people to care for us and teach us how to be in the world. As babies, we're programmed to seek out connections and to be attended to through our loud or quiet cries, our twinkling eyes, and our gurgles and giggles. We are born into a family under the guise that we will be taken care of and loved.

Unfortunately, that doesn't always happen. Some children are conceived and born unwanted and unwelcome. As an adult, you may have engaged in fun-filled unprotected sex, not thinking of the consequences. You may have wanted a baby to keep your partner around or to give you someone to love and be loved by. You may have been sexually abused and don't want a reminder of that traumatic event. There are multiple reasons a child may be conceived, yet once he or she is born, the adult present is responsible for his or her care.

There are so many challenges related to being a caregiver. These include being stretched and pulled when trying to navigate the ups and downs of life as an individual, possibly a couple, and then as a family. For starters, the caregiver is responsible for providing for the family's basic needs of food, shelter, and clothing. On top of these are the child's specific needs—emotional, social, physical, mental, and spiritual. These needs change as children go through the various ages and stages of life/development in conjunction with the caregiver's personal development. As a caregiver, every day is a challenge in creating balance in your self-care, marital/couple care, and family care while dealing with your extended family, work, community, society, and the world.

Depending on the level of dysfunction or disconnection you experienced as a child, the quality and style of your parenting will impact your current family dynamics. If your parents had been strict and punitive toward you as a child, you might be laid back and lenient or you might be overly involved and hover around your children. You might have been raised as a child "to be seen and not heard" so you might repeat this or do the opposite by giving your children too much of a say. If your parents weren't physically and/or emotionally available to you, there is a good chance you will not be physically or emotionally present for your children either.

The good news is that due to the resilience of children and their need for familial attachment, it is rarely too late to break these negative interactional patterns and create new ways of connecting as a family.

Several times I've heard caregivers say they want to do more or give more to their kids than they had themselves, only to repeat similar negative patterns from their childhoods. We may say to ourselves, "Oh, I'll never say that to my child" or "I would never do that when I have kids" only to experience sounding and acting just like our parents, especially in times of stress. I've also met several caregivers who missed opportunities to teach basic skills—for example, how to manage one's emotions, how to communicate, and how to resolve conflict. This often happens due to the caregiver's lack of exposure in learning these skills as well as personal issues or distractions in meeting the family's basic needs. Sometimes we forget that children are children and not little adults, leading us as caregivers to expect more from our children than may be realistic. At the same time, as caregivers we often want to look like "we have it all together" or "we can handle this by ourselves" so that others won't find fault or make fun of us. This sets us up to feel overwhelmed and to be at risk of: making poor choices such as saying or doing hurtful things toward unrelated persons, escaping with drugs or alcohol, and struggling with mental health issues such as depression and anxiety.

Please know, **all** caregivers struggle at different times with how to raise their children. Through no fault of our own, we all have personal or relational baggage, or both, in how we were raised. That baggage impacts how we parent. While raising your children day in and day out, you may question if you are making the right decisions or if there is something more you could be doing to help your child. This book will show you that there are innumerable ways to relate and engage with children to create the kind of relationships you want in life. Yet keep in mind as you progress through this book that **the quality of your interaction is more important than the activities themselves.**

I felt led to create this book after reading numerous parenting books, none of which were as simple and understandable as my clients needed them to be. My twenty-five-plus years of experience and training as a therapist taught me invaluable skills that I wanted to share with others.

A fascination with words and fonts led to exploring my dictionary and thesaurus for words to elaborate on the foundational caregiving concepts listed in this book. Words are intriguing in how they look as well as in how similar or different they are in their meaning. I believe in the power of words to build one up or tear one down.

As an artist, I felt led to add images to broaden the reader's use of the parenting concepts. Art-making in general has a way of helping us get in touch with our younger, more playful selves. You are encouraged to experiment with different mediums and to take risks with your creative process. I invite you to share your images as you feel comfortable with family, friends, or therapists. Display them in different places in your house as a reminder of who you are and who you want to be as a family.

Blessings and joy to all who celebrate the wonder of children and *being* human beings!

GETTING STARTED:
OVERVIEW OF THE A TO Z CONCEPTS

The A to Z concepts listed in this book highlight the needed familial qualities for building or rediscovering healthier family connections. Each concept was carefully selected based on my years of experience in helping families to stay together and promoting the healing of strained relationships. Before beginning with the activities, I'd suggest reading through the list below and selecting the concepts that most resonate with your present situation.

- **AFFIRMATION** speaks to a basic form of communication that focuses on the positives and the acceptance of someone for who he is.
- **BELONGING** refers to a child's basic need for attachment that imbues a sense of safety and security.
- **CONNECTION** acknowledges the child's need for her family to interact with each other as well as with the community for work, school, and recreation.
- **DEPENDABILITY** provides another essential layer of stability, emotionally and physically, for a child's development.
- **EMPOWERMENT** allows children to discover what they are capable of and what they have control of.
- **FLEXIBILITY** demonstrates for children the benefit of being adaptable to life's changes by bending rather than breaking, collapsing, or blowing up.
- **GUIDANCE** teaches your child about the world and how to live in it.
- **HOPEFULNESS** promotes the belief in unlimited possibilities for children and shines a light in dark places.
- **IDENTITY** speaks to your child about being true to who he is as an individual and taking chances to discover what feels right.
- **(Life Is a) JOURNEY** represents for your child the process of living daily life as being more important than a specific destination.
- **KINDLING Connections** responds to your child's sparks of interest by providing beneficial resources and support for ideas to flourish.

- **LOVING Unconditionally** shows unfailing commitment to your child through the ups and downs of life.

- **MEMORY-MAKING** helps children create a formal or informal documentation of daily and special events that will be cherished for a lifetime.

- **NURTURING GROWTH** supports the individual development of your child through planting seeds, weeding unhealthy growth nearby, and providing support as needed for the your child to reach for the sky.

- **OPEN-MINDEDNESS** expands your child's perception and acceptance of others, especially if their ideals are different or contrary to what you believe in.

- **PLAYFULNESS** invites caregivers to relate to children through play—the language through which children learn about themselves and the world.

- **QUALITY TIME** reflects a commitment to being together as a family; whether related to work or play—this time is more important than things.

- **ROLE MODELING** demonstrates how children imitate what they see and hear—the good and the bad.

- **STRUCTURE** holds the family unit together inside and out through the use of routines, expectations, and positive and/or negative consequences.

- **(Good) TOUCH** teaches children about healthy physical and emotional boundaries; it also meets a physical need for comfort and affection.

- **UNDERSTANDING** highlights the importance of putting ourselves in each other's shoes to make sense of the other's reality/experience.

- **VALUES** are foundational beliefs caregivers introduce to children that guide their words and actions on a daily basis.

- **WORK** speaks to the challenges we all face as individuals and as a family in experiencing a sense of accomplishment in life, whether physically, mentally, emotionally, and/or spiritually.

- **EXPRESSIONS** communicate our thoughts and feelings in the moment or after the fact to help both children and caregivers to be heard.

- **(Say) YES!** rewards children with a vote of trust and confidence in their ability to learn from their actions.

- **ZEST** celebrates the wonder of being alive and living more fully.

The ABCs

Affirmation

Speaks to a basic form of communication that focuses on the positives

and the acceptance of someone for who she is.

Show interest in and care for your child in the moment by —

    Looking into her eyes

    Rubbing her head when you pass by

    Holding her hand and requesting she squeeze your hand as hard as she can

Affirm your child's thoughts, feelings, and experiences by asking —

    "How hard was it for you to try something for the first time?"

    "What did it feel like when you _____?"

    "What are you looking forward to in starting a new school year?"

Show affirmation for how your child treated you by saying —

    "I enjoy seeing your smile the first thing in the morning."

    "I appreciate you being responsible by putting your belongings away without being asked."

    "I loved getting this card from you just because. It made my day."

Applaud and affirm your child by saying —

    "I am so proud of you for taking a risk by _____."

    "I appreciated seeing that you didn't give up when something was hard to do."

    "Good job in making a good choice by _____."

How do you show affirmation to your children?

_____

_____

_____

_____

Other A words to ponder and personalize:

accept	advocate	agree to disagree
attend	answer	apologize
applaud	appreciate	aspire
be accountable	acknowledge	adapt

Belonging

Refers to a child's basic need for attachment that imbues a sense of safety and security.

Let your child know he belongs by saying —

"I value your presence in my life."

"I feel more whole having you as part of my life."

"I look forward to being a part of you growing up."

Show your child belonging by —

Having special rituals to say good-bye, good night, and hello

Having time and space to be together

Getting things that interest, engage, and comfort him

Tell your child —

"I love you to the ends of the earth and beyond."

"I believe in you and want the best for you."

"I hope you have a better day."

Create a home environment that —

Welcomes your child to grow and develop through life's ages and stages

Is physically and emotionally safe (i.e., an environment that eliminates physical and verbal aggression, that allows access to activities based on your child's age and ability, that fosters a sense of respect for persons and property, and where caregivers speak and act in a manner they want their children to emulate)

Invites having a balance between work and play

How do you show belonging to your children?

_____

_____

_____

_____

Other B words to ponder and personalize:

build up	have beliefs	bolster
balance	celebrate birthdays	practice boundaries
bargain	give blessings	show bravery
be present physically and emotionally	bloom	build bridges

Connection

Acknowledges the child's need for her family to interact with each other

as well as with the community for work, school, and recreation.

Find ways to be with one another by —

    Playing together (e.g., games, toys, puppets, or dress up)

    Talking in silly voices and making silly faces

    Showing how to do something for the first time (e.g., cook, tie a shoe, ride a bike)

Tell your child —

    "I am looking forward to hearing about your day."

    "I am always here for you no matter what."

    "I want to know what you want or need from me."

Teach your child how to —

    Express thoughts and feelings in the moment or in reflection

    Take risks and learn new skills even when it feels scary or uncomfortable

    Get along with other people whether she likes them or not through tolerance and acceptance of differences; this includes some family members

Learn about your child —

    By asking, "How do you know that at your age?" without expecting a verbal answer

    By showing an interest in what she is telling or showing you

    By commenting about differences in her appearance or mood

How do you show a sense of connection to your children?

_____

_____

_____

_____

Other C words to ponder and personalize:

have courage	cherish	collaborate
show curiosity	chip in	be creative
celebrate	cuddle	be consistent
compromise	clarify	comfort
cheer	coach	compliment

Dependability

Provides another essential layer of stability,

emotionally and physically, for a child's development.

Let your child know you're dependable by saying —

"You can count on me to be there for you."

"I may make mistakes; however, I love you and want to learn from this experience."

"There may be times that work, traffic, or people get in the way, but that doesn't mean you aren't important to me."

Show your child dependability by —

Doing what you say you are going to do

Acting the way you want your child to act

Being there when he needs you—for the good times and the not-so-good times

Tell your child —

"I am sorry for _____" (if you make a mistake). "I didn't mean to _____."

"I want you to be able to trust what I say and do."

"Let me know if I ever hurt you without realizing it."

Create a home environment where —

Your children's basic needs are met on a daily basis

Your children can be kids and not worry about adult issues and responsibilities

Your children look forward to special occasions and time as a family

How do you show dependability to your children?

_____

_____

_____

_____

Other D words to ponder and personalize:

dance	review decision-making process	do
defend	discipline yourself	perform a duty
devote	display	dream

Empowerment

Allows children to discover what they are capable of and what they have control of.

Show your child that you believe in what she can do by —

> Giving her opportunities to do things by herself (e.g., pouring a drink or picking out clothes)

> Doing things side by side in order to teach something (e.g., cracking an egg, fixing a car, or folding clothes)

> Starting to let go so your child can do things on her own (e.g., riding a bike, getting dressed, tying her shoes)

Tell your child —

> "I know you can do this! I believe in you."

> "If it doesn't work out this time, you can learn from this and try again."

> "I know you have what it takes to _____."

Empower your child in the moment by —

> Inviting questions to promote learning and understanding

> Squeezing your child's hand and letting go

> Getting the needed supplies to complete her task

Let your child know —

> "Things don't always work out the first time, but don't give up."

> "Most things in life you need to work for. They won't just be given to you."

> "You are worth it. You are enough."

How do you show empowerment to your children?

_____

_____

_____

_____

Other E words to ponder and personalize:

educate	encounter	entertain
embrace	endure	be enthusiastic
empathize	engage in activities	have self-esteem
enable	enjoy	evaluate

Flexibility

Demonstrates for children the benefit of being adaptable to life's changes by bending rather than breaking, collapsing, or blowing up.

Show your child flexibility by —

> Stopping what you are doing and looking at him

> Modifying your daily schedule so you can spend more time with him

> Keeping your feelings in control when upset by an unexpected change

Tell your child —

> "There are some things in life you can control and change, and some things you need to learn to live with."

> "Sometimes we need to stop and change course."

> "It's okay to feel upset or disappointed when things don't work out the way you wanted."

Teach your child by —

> Making changes to your daily routine/schedule when needed for the benefit of your child or others

> Taking time to reflect on how you spend your time and energy

> Seeing the various possibilities in how to work something out from your child's point of view as well as from your perspective

Let your child know —

> "You are going to be okay even if things don't happen the way you wanted them to."

> "I believe in your ability to figure this out."

> "We are stronger when we bend like a tree, than if we just break apart."

How do you show flexibility to your children?

_____

_____

_____

_____

Other F words to ponder and personalize:

face each other	share feelings	forgive
family before phones	focus	fortify
be faithful	practice good finances	enjoy freedoms
be with family	be fond of	have fun

13

Guidance

Teaches your child about the world and how to live in it.

Teach your child guidance by —

Living the way you want her to behave

Discussing choices and actions she makes or wants to make

Seeking outside help when you aren't able to work something out by yourself

Tell your child —

"We as a family value _____ and hope you will too."

"I trust you will make a good decision in how you handle this situation."

"We are stronger when we help and support each other rather than when we handle things alone."

Show your child guidance by —

Asking for help when you don't understand something

Admitting you don't have all the answers

Standing up for what you believe in even when others don't agree or support you

Create a home environment that —

Limits distractions when you talk to each other

Promotes comfort and closeness in its seating (i.e., good touch and eye contact)

Respects people, space, and property through healthy boundaries and care

How do you show guidance to your children?

_____

_____

_____

_____

Other G words to ponder and personalize:

play games	follow the golden rule	have grace
understand your genealogy	show gratitude	glue that holds the family together
be generous	have goals	grow
give and take	go places	grieve losses

16

Hopefulness

Promotes the belief in unlimited possibilities for children and shines a light in dark places.

Show your child hopefulness by —

> Not giving up, and trying other ways to get what you want or need

> Looking for what is going well or right with this or other situations

> Taking risks and learning from your mistakes

Tell your child —

> "If at first you don't succeed, try, try again."

> "Life is full of good and bad people and experiences. It's up to you what you focus on."

> "There is a light at the end of the tunnel. I will believe it for you."

Teach your child how to —

> Pace themselves and take small steps to get what they want in the long run

> Be kind to themselves as they learn something new

> Cope during difficult times. As my mother always said, "This too shall pass."

Create a home environment where family members —

> Show support for one another during both joyous and uncertain/stressful times

> Focus more on the positives of life, whether in situations, people, or experiences

> Provide opportunities to figure things out, or to ask for help if needed

How do you show hopefulness to your children?

_____

_____

_____

_____

Other H words to ponder and personalize:

harmonize	enjoy family heirlooms	have humor
be healthy	be helpful	enjoy holidays
hear	be in a hierarchy	have a place to call home
have a good heart	know your history	be honest

Identity

Speaks to your child about being true to who he is as an individual

and taking chances to discover what feels right.

Let your child know how identity evolves by saying —

"I like seeing you try different things to see what feels right for you."

"It is important to be you."

"This is who we want to be as a family."

Show your child a sense of positive identity by —

Dressing and acting in a manner that feels comfortable to you

Asking questions and standing up for what you believe in, as well as showing respect for others' points of view

Accepting and taking care of your body as a woman or a man. In the process, you help your child to accept his physical appearance and develop a more positive self-image

Tell your child —

"There may be people who don't like you, but that doesn't mean there is anything wrong with you."

"You are special, being who you are."

"There is only one you, and I love you no matter what!"

Show interest in and care for your child's identity in the moment by —

Noticing and commenting when he dresses or talks differently

Offering to find and purchase items that interest him

Telling stories about favorite memories of him

How do you show identity to your children?

_____

_____

_____

_____

Other I words to ponder and personalize:

have ideas	be interdependent	inquire
imagine	know information	have insight
have intentions	inherit	inspire
include	show initiative	invest

(Life Is a) Journey

Represents for your child the process of living daily life as being

more important than a specific destination.

Show your child life is a journey by —

> Making short-term and long-term plans for yourself and for your family

> Talking about the ups and downs of life as part of being alive

> Celebrating transition times and accomplishments

Tell your child —

> "Taking small steps will help you get where you want to go in life."

> "You have many choices and roads you can choose from for work and for play."

> "You are not alone. We are in this together."

Teach your child —

> To solve problems or conflicts when things aren't working out or feeling right to you

> Even if you make a wrong turn or a mistake, you can learn from it and move on

> Taking time to enjoy the moment is more important than focusing on the destination

Let your child know —

> "I support what you want to do as long as you or no one else will get hurt."

> "I admire your commitment to achieving your goals."

> "I am here for you if you need help along the way."

How do you show being on a journey to your children?

_____

_____

_____

_____

Other J words to ponder and personalize:

| join | journal | juggle |
| joke | practice joy | jump start |

Kindling (Connections)

Responds to your child's sparks of interest by providing

beneficial resources and support for ideas to flourish.

Show your child how to kindle a connection by —

Taking the time to just be together as a family

Asking questions about what your child thinks and feels about certain things

Finding ways to reinforce her personality and interests

Tell your child —

"Sometimes you need to take small steps to get what you want."

"I believe in what you want to do."

"I know you have what it takes to get through this difficult time."

Teach your child the value of —

Not giving up on relationships when things get too hard

Creating plans with specific family members and acting upon them

Believing in the goodness present in each family member

Kindle a connection with your child by —

Offering work or play activities, and observing how she interacts with others

Seeing how she responds to challenges, transitions, or change

Observing what motivates her to start a project and not give up

How do you show ways of kindling connection to your children?

_____

_____

_____

_____

Other K words to ponder and personalize:

show kindness	expand knowledge	let kids be kids
kiss	knuckle down if needed	cherish kindred spirits
nurture kinship	offer kudos	keep the faith

Loving (Unconditionally)

Shows unfailing commitment to your child through the ups and downs of life.

Show your child loving unconditionally by —

> Learning what feels like "love" to your child (e.g., physical touch, gifts, quality time, acts of service, and/or words of affirmation according to Gary Chapman's *Five Love Languages*)

> Treating each other the way you would like to be treated—the Golden Rule

> Respecting and accepting when he doesn't like something, with little to no questioning

Tell your child —

> "I love you to the ends of the earth and beyond."

> "I love seeing you smile."

> "I love seeing how much you care for your pet."

Teach your child —

> There are numerous ways to show and feel love toward oneself and others

> To speak up, if he feels mistreated by anyone—family, friends, teachers, or strangers

> How to get help if he feels unsafe or mistreated by others

Create a home environment where family members —

> Show respect for each other's personal space and identity

> Give affection in a manner that feels comfortable to each family member

> Learn to enjoy each other by focusing on the positive and what is special about how each person acts and talks

How do you show your children how to love unconditionally?

_____

_____

_____

_____

Other L words to ponder and personalize:

learn your child's language	do laundry together	lift up
laugh	light the way	lighten the load
let go	understand your legacy	listen
learn something new	enjoy leisure time	live life

Memory-Making

Helps children create a formal or informal documentation of daily

and special events that will be cherished for a lifetime.

Teach your children the value of memory-making by —

 Recording everyday or special events with photos or videos

 Looking back at old photos and telling stories about them

 Enjoying memorable things as a family such as vacations, parties, and celebrations

Tell your child —

 "I remember the first time I held you. . . ."

 "I remember seeing you learn to _____ and you didn't give up."

 "I remember how proud I was of you when you _____."

Show your child memory-making by —

 Spending time taking pictures, developing them, and putting them in an album

 Recalling family or personal joys and struggles

 Providing your child with a camera for her to take pictures of special moments or everyday events, with or without you

Let your child know —

 "You get to write your life story however you want to."

 "You have the power to rewrite what you remember or want out of life."

 "You help to create positive memories that you will cherish forever."

How do you show memory-making to your children?

_____

_____

_____

_____

Other M words to ponder and personalize:

magnify the positives	mend broken ties	have a mission
make meaning	mark milestones	enjoy the moment
have manners	be mindful	motivate
enjoy mealtimes	mirror feelings	muddle through

Nurturing Growth

Supports the individual development of your child through planting seeds, weeding unhealthy growth nearby, and providing support as needed for the your child to reach for the sky.

Nurture your child's growth by —

Paying attention to what interests and motivates him

Acknowledging specific things your child says or does that you value

Providing opportunities to do things that reinforce your child's interests and abilities

Tell your child —

"You have the ability to do what you want to do if you put the time and energy into it."

"You need to decide what feels right for you and not do just what other people tell you."

"You deserve to have good things in your life."

Teach your child the value of —

Finding a silver lining when the skies grow dark

Having a positive attitude, so he can feel better about himself and life

Believing in his abilities, so that he can feel good about himself and how he gets along with others

Create a home environment where family members are —

Able to try new things and feel encouraged for their efforts

Able to show off their work and feel proud of it

Supported so they can talk about what feels good and what doesn't

How do you show your children how to nurture growth?

_____

_____

_____

_____

Other N words to ponder and personalize:

name	know your neighborhood	being normal is an illusion
navigate	be nice	be nonjudgmental
negotiate	nip negativity	nourish

Open-Mindedness

Expands your child's perception and acceptance of others,

especially if their ideals are different or contrary to what you believe in.

Show your child open-mindedness by —

> Listening to people you may not like or agree with

> Trying new things—for example, food, technology, activities, or music

> Going new places, such as restaurants, parks, museums, or cities

Tell your child —

> "There are a lot of different ways to do things."

> "There is no **ONE** right way to do anything."

> "There are a lot of people you may agree with or disagree with. And that is okay."

Teach your child the value of —

> Agreeing to disagree

> Learning about other people and cultures

> Accepting and tolerating others' differences (e.g., beliefs, dress, customs, etc.)

Let your child know —

> "You decide if you want to make friends or enemies of the people you meet in life."

> "What may feel good and right to you may not feel good to someone else."

> "There are more possibilities in looking through a window than a closed door."

How do you show open-mindedness to your children?

_____

_____

_____

_____

Other O words to ponder and personalize:

observe	be open	take ownership
overcome obstacles	be optimistic	create order

Playfulness

Invites caregivers to relate to children through play—

the language through which children learn about themselves and the world.

Show your child playfulness by —

>Joining her and doing what she enjoys, versus expecting her to do only what you want or feel comfortable with

>Getting down on the floor and playing with her

>Smiling and laughing when she's being silly

Tell your child —

>"I enjoy watching you _____ with your toys."

>"I like seeing you smile and laugh when we _____."

>"I appreciate how you use your imagination when you _____."

Teach your child the value of —

>Sharing and taking turns while playing together

>Clarifying ground rules before the game starts

>Having fun together, because it is more important than winning

Create a home environment where your child can —

>Explore and experiment during playtime

>Feel encouraged to try new things or to be different

>Have space to store and move around playthings

How do you show playfulness to your children?

_____

_____

_____

_____

Other P words to ponder and personalize:

make peace with the past	plan	prevent problems
be patient	problem-solve	be open to possibilities
persevere	process interactions	understand your power
protect	respect privacy	be present

Quality Time

Reflects a commitment to being together as a family; whether related to work or play—

this time is more important than things.

Show your child the concept of quality time by —

> Taking time out of your busy schedule to do things together
>
> Consistently scheduling time with him on a weekly basis and keeping it sacred
>
> Canceling or not scheduling things during times set aside for you both

Tell your child —

> "I value spending time with you."
>
> "I look forward to when we get to _____ together."
>
> "I welcome ideas about how you would like to spend our time together."

Teach your child the value of —

> Taking time for what is important to you
>
> Doing what you say you are going to do
>
> Spending time together, which is more important than getting or having things

Show interest in and care for your child by —

> Going to special events at school or in the community
>
> Doing things your child likes to do even if you don't feel comfortable or enjoy the activities
>
> Providing opportunities to reinforce your child's interests or strengths

How do you show quality time to your children?

_____

_____

_____

_____

Other Q words to ponder and personalize:

make-up from quarrels and quibbles	ask questions	quit making excuses
make a family quilt	have quirks	be quiet

Role Modeling

Demonstrates how children imitate what they see and hear—the good and the bad.

Show your child role modeling by —

> Talking and behaving in a manner you want your child to emulate

> Pointing out others who are making good or not-so-good choices as examples to learn from

> Admitting when you, as the adult, make a mistake so you can apologize and move on

Tell your child —

> "You have the power to influence how people think of you and treat you."

> "Other people see what you do and may look up to you. When this happens what do you want them to see?"

> "That person just made a good choice by _____ (or) set a good example by _____."

Teach your child the value of —

> Asking questions if she doesn't understand why things are done in a certain way

> Showing respect toward others who are different from your family

> Treating others the way you'd like to be treated

Create a home environment where family members —

> Reinforce each other's good choices and decisions

> Pay attention and show consideration toward people, animals, and things

> Encourage one another to talk about things they like or don't like

How do you show being a role model to your children?

_____

_____

_____

_____

Other R words to ponder and personalize:

read together	reconcile differences	be reliable
reassure	be resourceful	rewrite one's life story
rise above	have resilience	be responsible
practice rituals	reinforce good choices	be respectful

Structure

Holds the family unit together inside and out through the use of routines, expectations,

and positive and/or negative consequences.

Show your child structure by —

> Having a consistent daily routine and expectations for how to get through the day
>
> Modifying your expectations to match his age and stage of development
>
> Being present and supporting him in learning how to do things for himself

Tell your child —

> "You need to learn to do certain things that will help you at school and in the future."
>
> "You may not like doing things this way; however, when you are on your own you can do it your way."
>
> "If you don't like or understand how to do something, please let me know so we can work it out."

Teach your child the value of —

> Order, so he can find things when he wants them, such as shoes, toys, and clothes
>
> Giving and taking as part of family life
>
> Scheduling or making lists, or both, to get things done, whether related to work or play

Create a home environment where caregivers —

> Allow time for kids to be kids
>
> Create a balance between work and play to meet all family members' needs
>
> Demonstrate consistency and care, thus providing a sense of safety and stability

How do you show structure to your children?

_____

_____

_____

_____

Other S words to ponder and personalize:

appreciate safety and security	be spiritual	be steadfast
show up	tell stories	stop and think
be silly	practice sportsmanship	have self-compassion
be respectful of space	understand stages	support

(Good) Touch

Teaches children about healthy physical and emotional boundaries;

it also meets a physical need for comfort and affection.

Show your child appropriate levels of touch by —

> Giving hugs, kisses, backrubs, or cuddles to match your child's comfort level
>
> Respecting your child's wishes if she asks not to be touched
>
> Asking if she would like to be hugged or receive other forms of affection

Tell your child —

> "Please let me know if anyone ever touches you in a manner you don't like."
>
> "I love our time together when we _____ before going to bed."
>
> "Let me know if you ever need a hug."

Teach your child the value of —

> Being able to say "no" if she isn't comfortable with how someone is touching her
>
> Feeling good about her body and treating it with respect and care
>
> Speaking up about what feels good and what doesn't feel good when being touched, as well as the concepts of private parts and who is allowed to see or touch them (e.g., a doctor)

Create a home environment where family members —

> Use touch to show love and respect even if someone is upset
>
> Feel safe and secure in their own spaces
>
> Learn to manage their feelings so as not to be physically hurtful toward others

How do you show good touch to your children?

_____

_____

_____

_____

Other T words to ponder and personalize:

treasure each other	be thankful	tolerate
take turns	be thoughtful	toast accomplishments
tell the truth	enjoy time together	trust
practice teamwork	enjoy some TLC	tune in

Understanding

Highlights the importance of putting ourselves in each other's shoes

to make sense of the other's reality/experience.

Show your child understanding by —

> Taking the time to find out his thoughts and feelings

> Focusing on what he may need from you more than your feelings at that moment

> Being willing to make changes if needed to help deal with a situation

Tell your child —

> "I want to hear what you think and feel about _____."

> "I want to understand what you are going through."

> "I am interested in hearing about _____."

Teach your child the value of —

> Looking at situations from different points of view

> Respecting different ways of seeing and doing things

> Agreeing to disagree on certain topics

Let your child know —

> "What you think and feel is important to me."

> "No matter what, I will always have time for you to talk to me."

> "I will accept and love you no matter what."

How do you show understanding to your children?

_____

_____

_____

_____

Other U words to ponder and personalize:

use an umbrella (against life's storms)	practice unconditional love	unplug technology
unify	speak in unison	unload troubles
unite	be unique	look up

43

Values

Are foundational beliefs caregivers introduce to children that guide their words and actions on a daily basis.

Show your child values by —

> Living according to what you believe in (e.g., education, trust, and structure)
>
> Teaching her the significance of having standards for living
>
> Modifying your actions if you learned there is a better way to do something

Tell your child —

> "Your actions speak louder than words."
>
> "People remember first impressions, so consider how you want people to think of you."
>
> "These are the values we are choosing to live by now; however, as you get older you can decide which values you want to live by."

Teach your child the value of —

> Having multiple choices in how she spends her time and energy
>
> Deciding what feels right in how she is treated by others
>
> Living according to what she believes in and not allowing others to sway her

Create a home environment where caregivers —

> Use and display things that match your family values (e.g., books and sports ribbons or trophies)
>
> Learn about and monitor what your children are involved in or interested in (e.g., TV, computer, cell phones, games, music, books, magazines, peers, school subjects and activities)
>
> Reinforce good choices related to living by your family's values

How do you show the importance of values with your children?

_____

_____

_____

_____

Other V words to ponder and personalize:

take a vacation	be visible	use your voice
use variation	have vision	vote
venture out	vanish negativity	be vulnerable

Work

Speaks to the challenges we all face as individuals and as a family in experiencing a sense of accomplishment in life, whether physically, mentally, emotionally, and/or spiritually.

Show your child the proper way to work by —

>   Balancing work and play as well as adult and child time

>   Having him be open to learning and trying new ways to get a job done

>   Teaching, step by step, how to do things that develop his skills

Tell your child —

>   "If at first you don't succeed, try, try again."

>   "It's okay to ask questions or ask for help if you don't know how to do something."

>   "Some things take more time to learn and to do."

Teach your child the value of —

>   Taking your time to do the job right and feeling good about it

>   Learning your effort at a task is more important than the outcome

>   Admitting when you did something wrong and trying to fix it

Let your child know —

>   "I believe in your ability to _____."

>   "I am here for you if you need help with _____."

>   "It's not possible or realistic to be good at everything. We each have strengths in different areas."

How do you show your children the right way to work?

_____

_____

_____

_____

Other W words to ponder and personalize:

having wants vs. needs	weather the storms of life	know that winning isn't everything
be warmhearted	weave memories	be willing
watch and learn	wipe the slate clean	wonder
we are one	be workable	wait your turn

eXpressions

Communicate our thoughts and feelings in the moment or after the fact

to help both children and caregivers to be heard.

Show your child positive self-eXpression by —

> Having your face and body match how you feel inside
>
> Being silly and childlike if the situation suits this behavior
>
> Speaking up to share your thoughts and feelings

Tell your child —

> "I am interested in hearing what you have to say even if I don't agree."
>
> "I enjoy seeing you _____ when you are feeling happy."
>
> "I want to know if you are feeling sad or angry because I care about you."

Teach your child the value of —

> Being honest about what she is thinking and feeling
>
> Letting others know if something doesn't look or feel right
>
> Learning to express herself, rather than keeping feelings inside or lashing out

Create a home environment where family members —

> Have daily conversations about past, present, or future people and events
>
> Support compassion, vulnerability, and sharing of uncomfortable feelings
>
> Welcome disagreements or differences of opinion to promote understanding

How do you show eXpressions to your children?

_____

_____

_____

_____

Other X words to ponder and personalize:

use an eXample	eXpect change	eXplore
eXchange ideas and things	eXperience	connect with eXtended family
be eXcited	eXperiment	eXpect the uneXpected
eXercise	eXplain	be eXtraordinary

(Say) Yes!

Rewards children with a vote of trust and confidence in their ability to learn from their actions.

Show your child you are saying "yes" by —

    Giving him the choice to do more than what he may think he is capable of

    Agreeing to do something in a different way; there is no *ONE* "right way"

    Being clear about what you are agreeing to and following through

Tell your child —

    "You have a right to say 'yes' or 'no' when choosing to do certain things."

    "It's okay to not do what everyone else is doing if you don't agree with it. There may be positive or negative consequences depending on what you choose."

    Depending on your child's age and maturity level... "You can choose what feels right for you to do when _____."

Teach your child the value of —

    Making decisions for himself

    Speaking up about what feels right and good

    Saying "no" if he doesn't have the time, energy, or interest to do something

Let your child know —

    "You will never be able to please everybody, so do what you need to do for you."

    "You have a right to stand up for what you believe in, even if others disagree."

    "I appreciate when you choose things that suit who you are as a person."

How do you say "yes" to your children?

_____

_____

_____

_____

Other Y words to ponder and personalize:

yawn (it's okay to be tired)	yearn for more	yell every once in a while
year	learn from your yesterdays	yield

Zest

Celebrates the wonder of being alive and living more fully.

Show your child zest by —

Having a sense of wonder and curiosity about life and the world—its science, diversity, and people

Taking better care of yourself physically, emotionally, mentally, and spiritually so you will be more present with your child as she grows up

Celebrating significant transitions and accomplishments with fun, family-friendly gatherings

Tell your child —

"It makes my day to see you smile and be so energetic."

"I enjoy hearing you ask questions to better understand things."

"I look forward to going places and doing things with you."

Teach your child the value of —

Taking responsibility for how you care for your body, mind, and spirit

Not giving up even when things get hard

Supporting yourself through struggles and the process of fulfilling dreams

Create a home environment where caregivers —

Plan and celebrate special events (e.g., births, birthdays, and graduations)

Show they're proud of who they are, both as individuals and as a family

Welcome silliness, laughter, and praise as well as questions, heartfelt expressions, and tears

How do you show zest with your children?

_____

_____

_____

_____

Other Z words to ponder and personalize:

be zany	have zing	zero in on joy
be zippy	be in the zone	nurture zeal

HOW TO USE THE
A TO Z COLORING PAGES

The coloring pages in this section give you and your family the chance to further personalize the ABC book experience. The following list provides gentle reminders for how to use these special pages:

- Decide which order you'd like to do the coloring pages; my recommendation is to focus on the image that matches the concept (or concepts) that you read about earlier in the book

- You can either keep the book intact as you color the pages, or rip out the pages as you work on them

- Make copies of the pages if other family members would like to join in

- Decorate the images however you would like whether **inside or outside of the lines** with a variety of mediums such as paints (e.g., watercolor, tempra, payons, watercolor pencils), drawing materials (e.g., black lead pencils, fat or thin markers, colored pencils, pastels, cray-pas), collage materials (e.g., magazine pictures, photographs, memorabilia, nature items) and assorted scissors for cutting out the collage images.

- Modify and personalize each image as you see fit with words, pictures, colors, textures, and shapes

- Allow your playful self to enjoy this creative process with no judgment—remember the joy and wonder of making art "just because"

- Hang your pictures on your walls or refrigerator to remind yourself of who you are or want to be as a family **OR** frame the pictures and give them as gifts **OR** make a scrapbook **OR** color the page and cut it out to paste on another piece of paper

- Journal more by adding more reflections and experiences such as: my family shows _____ by _____, _____ **OR** I feel _____ when I _____.

- Talk to family, friends, and/or a mental health professional about your experiences with the prescriptive tools and coloring pages

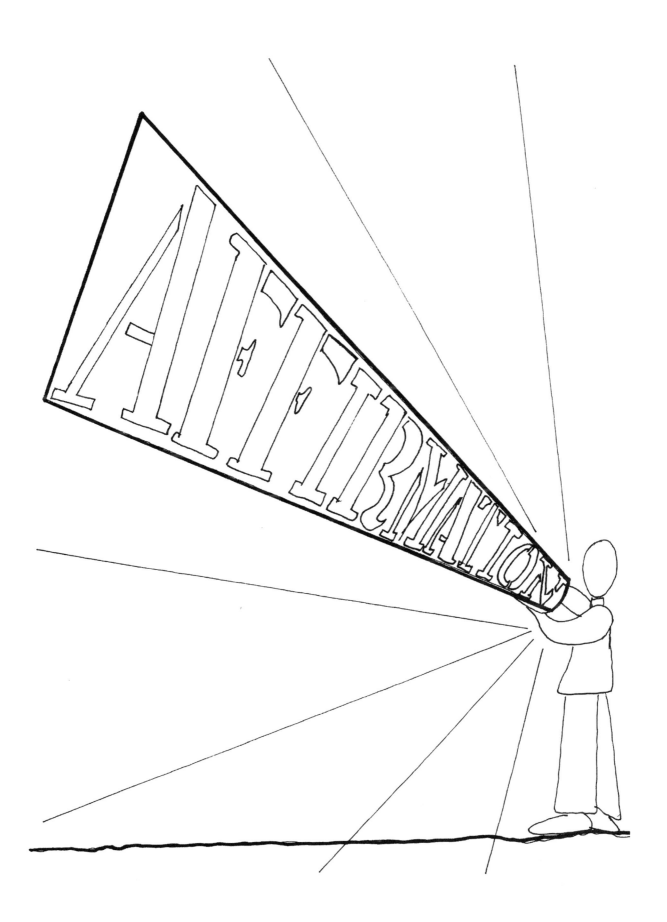

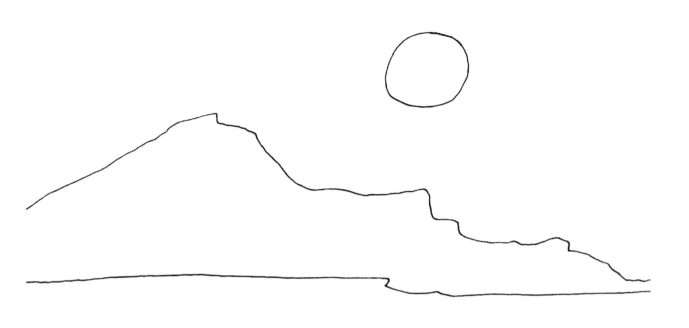

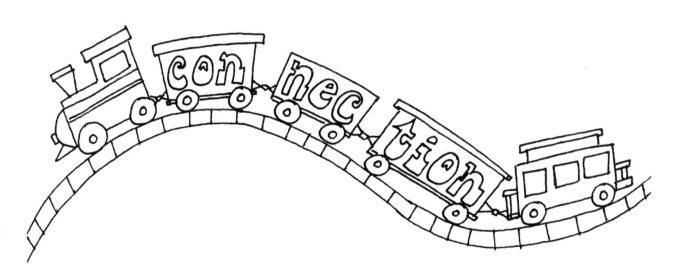

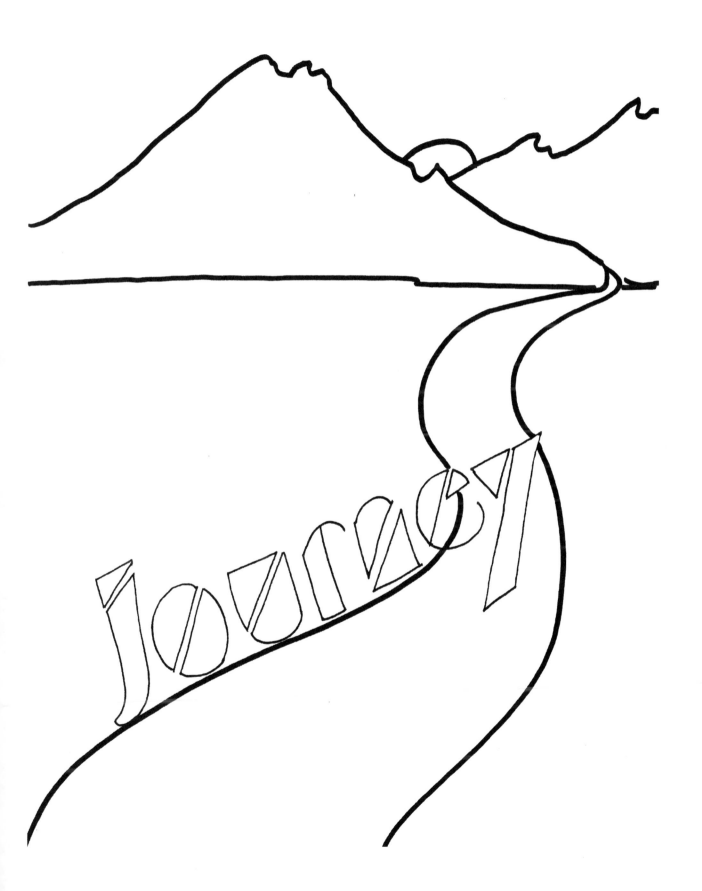

Memory-making

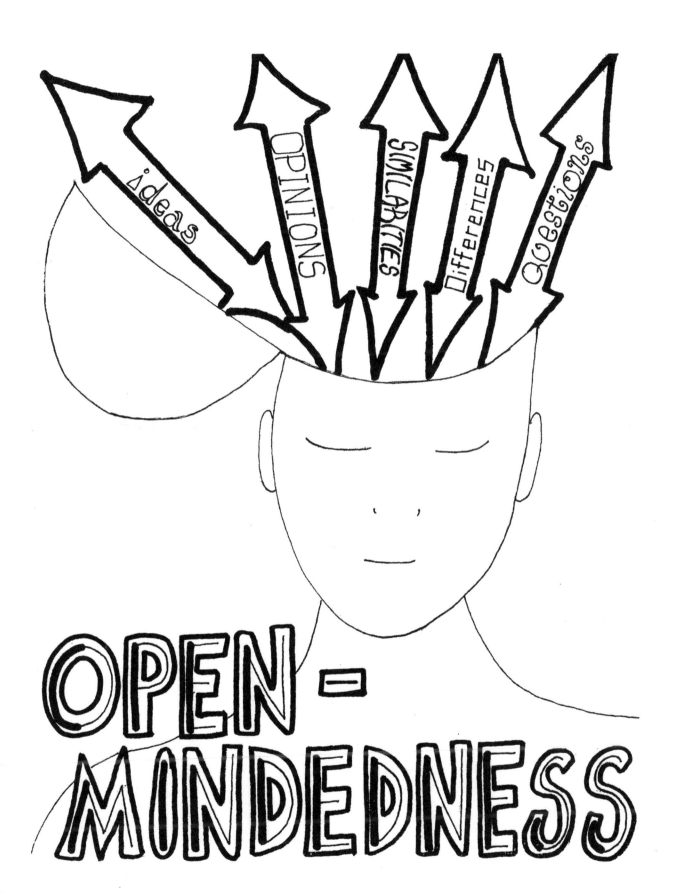

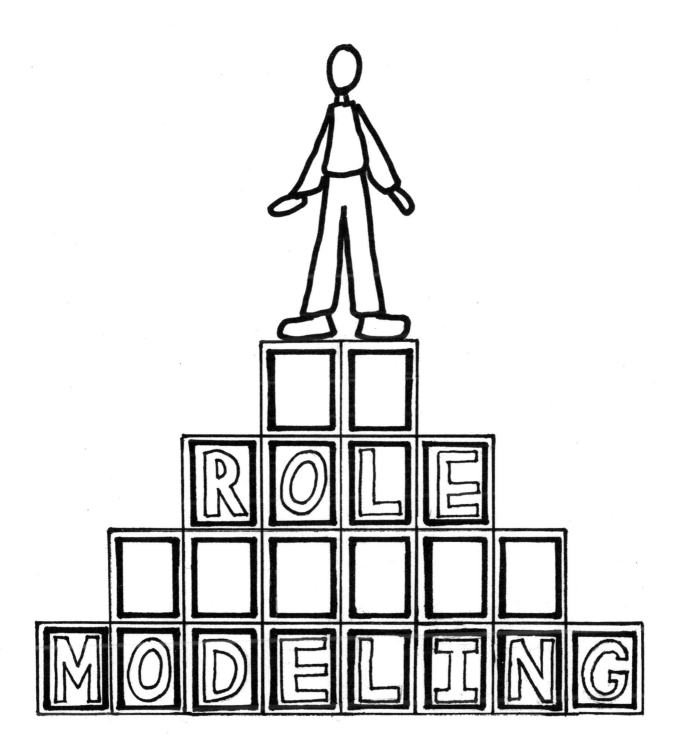

ENDING THOUGHTS

I hope you have enjoyed this time learning more about yourself and what you want for your family. Please know—**there is no right way to be a family**. Life in general is an ongoing process of ups and downs as we learn to cope with the storms of life. Living successfully often becomes a matter of whether you learn to go with the flow by riding the waves and battening down the hatches, **or** if you choose to go against the current and risk taking on water, running aground, or abandoning your ship. It is up to you. Just know that whatever you decide, you're not alone. We are made to learn from each other's experiences.

As a caregiver, you may be working to provide better experiences than you had as a child, yet you may also find yourself entrenched in negative patterns and behaviors. At these times we benefit from outside resources to help us regain perspective. This past year I discovered a book that spoke to my challenge of living a more authentic life, called *Daring Greatly* by Brené Brown. It asks parents: "Are you the adult you want your child to grow up to be?" The book's reflections on parenting and living wholeheartedly enriched my life. Perhaps Brown's question will speak to you as well. Remember—you are creating a legacy for your children and your children's children. You have more power and know-how than you may realize to make a difference in your children's lives.

Over the course of my career I have been honored to work with multiple families who were willing to take the risk to see and do things differently. By working together, we made it through difficult times and cleared away *some* of the negative baggage from the past. Note I said only "*some*," as there are always things to learn and work on in life. Overall, the families and I found new ways to experience and enjoy being a family, and were often able to evoke the magic of rediscovering their connections as a unit.

As you continue to rediscover your family, may you learn to have **grace** with yourself. I recently read "Stars can't shine without darkness." May this experience continue to bring light and joy into your life.

ADDITIONAL RESOURCES

Books

Ackerly, Rick. *The Genius in Every Child: Encouraging Character, Curiosity, and Creativity in Children* (Guilford, CT: Globe Pequot Press, 2012).

Bailey, Becky A. *I Love Your Rituals* (New York, NY: Harper Collins, 2000).

Brown, Brené. *Daring Greatly: How the Courage to Be Vulnerable Transforms the Way We Live, Love, Parent, and Lead* (New York, NY: Avery, 2015).

Chapman, Gary. *The Five Love Languages* (Chicago, IL: Northfield Press, 2004).

Clark, Jean I. and Connie Dawson. *Growing Up Again: Parenting Ourselves, Parenting Our Children* (Center City, MN: Hazelden, 1998).

Foster Cline, Foster, MD and Jim Fay. *Parenting with Love and Logic: Teaching Children Responsibility* (Colorado Springs, CO: Pinon, 1990).

Elkind, David. *The Power of Play: Learning What Comes Naturally* (Philadelphia, PA: De Capo Press, 2007).

Ginsburg, Kenneth R. with Martha M. Jablow. *A Parent's Guide to Building Resilience in Children and Teens: Giving Kids Roots and Wings* (Elk Grove Village, IL: American Academy of Pediatrics, 2006).

Nelsen, Jane. *Positive Discipline* (New York, NY: Ballantine Books, 2006).

SARK—Journal and Playbook (Berkeley, CA: Celestial Arts, 1993).

Smith, Keri. *How to Be an Explorer of the World: Portable Life Museum* (New York, NY: Perigee Books, 2008).

Tsabary, Shefali, PhD. *The Conscious Parent: Transforming Ourselves, Empowering Our Children* (Vancouver, British Columbia: Namaste Publishing, 2010).

Magazines and Websites

Magazines: *Family Circle, Family Fun, National Geographic for Kids, Parents, Seeing the Everyday.*

Websites: *Creative with Kids: The Art of Joyful Parenting, Hand in Hand: Nurturing the Parent-Child Connection, THRIVE.* Also search "play sites for kids" in your local area or state.

Play Sites

Various play sites—Let's Pretend in Middletown, PA; The State Museum of Pennsylvania in Harrisburg, PA; Hands on House in Lancaster, PA; The North Museum in Lancaster, PA; The Whitaker Center in Harrisburg, PA; Tumble Town at Colonial Park Mall in Harrisburg, PA; MOMS Club; MOPS; local libraries in your area (sign out educational play kits from the kids' section).

Mental Health Services

Various mental health services—Counseling agencies that provide individual, couples, and/or family therapy (search online for *Psychology Today* or MH agencies in your area).

SPECIAL THANKS

I would like to start by saying thanks to my family, friends, and therapist for believing in me and supporting the process of creating this book. Thanks to my partner, Debra, for your patience and encouragement as I have pursued my education and career as an artist and a therapist. Thanks to Terri Williams for helping me to take better care of myself and also for helping me to discover my gifts as an artist and a writer. Thanks to my parents for being proud of me for following through with this overall project.

I extend a special thanks to the numerous families whom I have had the honor of working with over these past twenty-five-plus years. You all inspired me to give back some of what I have learned, as well as taught me the power of transformation and grace.

I am grateful to PA Counseling Services/BHRS and Family-Based (FB) Programs for providing the opportunity to work with families and help them stay together and improve how they relate as a family. I thank Erin Tanner, my fellow FB therapist, for giving me ideas on how to improve the art images I created for the book. I thank Tara Byers, my former clinical supervisor, for her clinical input regarding this book. I have had multiple clinical supervisors, co-therapists, and FB trainers at work and graduate school who have enhanced my skills as a FB therapist—thanks to you, Jim Wanner, Harry Cook, Roger Beardmore, Sandy Holland, Josh Irvine, Wayne Jones, Marion Lindblad-Goldberg, and the Marywood University staff (Art Therapy Program, 1996-1999). I also thank Kasey Cox of From My Shelf Books in Wellsboro, Pennsylvania, for providing consultation about the publishing process. A special thanks to Nancy Eshelman, from PennLive, who helped me with the first edit of this book. Thanks too to Colleen McDonnell for her final edit as a mother of four children and fellow MH professional.

I would like to thank my past instructors and mentors (Wellsboro School District, Messiah College, Millersville University, Pennsylvania School of Art & Design, Lancaster Art Association, Marywood University, Penn State-Harrisburg, Shippensburg University-Dixon Center, Bethany Children's Home, Universalist Unitarian Church-Midwife Project, Stampington Press publications, and Life Is Good Playmakers). You helped me advance my education and skills as an artist and a therapist. I am thankful to my co-facilitators and participants in The Artemis Project for their engaging of women in creative activities to nurture their bodies, minds, and spirits. Thanks to Anne Moore from The Artemis Project, who gave me some writing and image pointers. I am also grateful to Jamie Julianna of Phoenix Pottery Studio for teaching me how to center myself and accept the creative process no matter how it turns out, as well as to follow one's dreams and take risks with one's livelihood.

I extend a special thank you to the Hillcrest Media Group and Langdon Street Press teams for helping to publish this book.

I am appreciative of all the previously listed authors and many more authors and artists, for having the courage to enter the arena of book publishing and sharing your knowledge and life experiences.

ABOUT THE AUTHOR

Betsy L. Stone lives in Harrisburg, Pennsylvania, with her partner of twenty-eight years and two cats. She graduated from Messiah College in 1986 with a BA in psychology and from Marywood University in 1999 with an MA in art therapy. She has worked in the mental health field for over twenty-five years, specializing in treating children and families. As of July 2014, Betsy received confirmation for Licensure as a Professional Counselor (LPC). She presently works at a local outpatient clinic in Harrisburg. This book is the first of many potential projects that will benefit both families and therapists.